SCIENCE AROUND US

Magnetism

By Darlene R. Stille

THE CHILD'S WORLD®
CHANHASSEN, MINNESOTA

Published in the United States of America by The Child's World®
PO Box 326, Chanhassen, MN 55317-0326
800-599-READ
www.childsworld.com

Content Adviser:
Mats Selen, PhD,
Professor of Physics,
University of Illinois,
Urbana, Illinois

Photo Credits:
Cover: Corbis
Interior: Bettmann/Corbis: 30-top, 30-middle, 30-bottom; Corbis: 6 (Randy Faris),
7, 9 (Roger Ressmeyer), 14, 18, 26 (James Leynse), 27 (Chase Swift); Custom Medical
Stock Photo: 15; Getty Images: 16 (Hulton|Archive), 22 (Time Life Pictures/Henry
Groskinsky); NASA/Marshall Space Flight Center: 16; Photo Researchers: 21 (Alex
Bartel), 24 (CC Studio); PictureQuest: 8 (Ron Elmy/firstlight), 11 (John Yurka/Index
Stock Imagery), 12 (Spencer Grant/PhotoEdit); Visuals Unlimited: 5 (Larry
Stepanowicz), 23 (Pegasus).

The Child's World®: Mary Berendes, Publishing Director

Editorial Directions, Inc.: E. Russell Primm, Editorial Director; Pam Rosenberg, Line
Editor; Katie Marsico, Assistant Editor; Matt Messbarger, Editorial Assistant; Susan
Hindman, Copy Editor; Susan Ashley, Proofreader; Peter Garnham, Olivia Nellums, and
Katherine Trickle, Fact Checkers; Tim Griffin/IndexServ, Indexer; Cian Laughlin
O'Day, Photo Researcher; Linda S. Koutris, Photo Selector

The Design Lab: Kathleen Petelinsek, Design and Page Production

Library of Congress Cataloging-in-Publication Data
Stille, Darlene R.
  Magnetism / by Darlene R. Stille.
    v. cm. — (Science around us)
Includes bibliographical references and index.
Contents: Discovering magnets—The shapes of magnets—Magnetic poles or a mysteri-
ous force—Magnetic fields or the power around a magnet—Making magnets—Using
magnets.
  ISBN 1-59296-222-X (lib. bdg. : alk. paper) 1. Magnetism—Juvenile literature.
[1. Magnetism. 2. Magnets.] I. Title. II. Science around us (Child's World (Firm))
  QC753.7.S73 2005
  538—dc22   2003027226

TABLE OF CONTENTS

CHAPTER ONE

DISCOVERING MAGNETS

Long ago in ancient Greece, a shepherd was walking on a hillside. Suddenly, it was hard for him to lift his feet. Something was pulling on his boots. What could it be?

He stopped and dug down in the ground. There he found a type of rock. He tested the rock on his boots. The rock was pulling on the iron nails in his boots.

This is a good story, but no one knows if it is true. The rock the shepherd found is called **lodestone.** A **mineral** called magnetite makes up lodestone. Magnetite is a natural magnet. The word *magnet* comes from a place in Greece called Magnesia.

Historians think that both the ancient Greeks and the ancient Chinese discovered that lodestone could pull on iron. They found

Iron filings stick to a lodestone, a rock made from the mineral magnetite.

that it would pull on some materials but not others. Lodestone

would pull on nails and tools made of iron, but not feathers, straw,

or cloth. Because of this, iron and some other metals are consid-

ered **magnetic materials.** Feathers, straw, cloth, concrete,

A feather is a nonmagnetic material because it is not attracted to magnets.

and rubber are **nonmag-netic materials.**

People then learned how to make metal into magnets. When they rubbed iron with lodestone, the iron became a magnet. Ancient people probably thought it was fun to play with magnets. They had no idea what magnets really were or what caused the mysterious pulling force.

Thousands of years after magnets were discovered, scientists learned about the power of magnets. In the 1800s, they discovered that magnetism is part of a great force of nature. Magnetism is a force that attracts iron, nickel, cobalt, and mixtures of some metals. Scientists learned how to make powerful magnets out of

certain metals. They learned how to make magnets do work. Now,

there are magnets in many of the things you use every day.

Many of the appliances you use in your home each day, such as this dishwasher,
have parts that contain magnets which help make them work.

CHAPTER TWO

THE SHAPES OF MAGNETS

Maybe you have a magnet on your refrigerator door. The magnet sticks to the metal door and holds notes and pictures. Refrigerator magnets are flat.

Magnets come in many other shapes. Horseshoe magnets are U-shaped. Bar magnets are long and straight. Magnets can be shaped like stars, circles, squares, diamonds, and other things.

No matter what the shape is, all magnets have two ends. The ends are called poles. All magnets have a north pole and a south pole. Poles give magnets their power to pull on iron nails in boots or stick to refrigerator doors.

Do you use magnets to hold things on your refrigerator door?

THE MAGNETIC COMPASS

A simple compass has a magnetic needle. The needle always points toward the north no matter which way you turn. A compass can keep you from getting lost. You can use a compass when you go hiking and when you go sailing. Maybe your family car has a compass onboard.

People first learned how to make a compass sometime in the 1000s or 1100s. Historians are not sure who made the first compass. It may have been made by the Chinese, by the Arabs, or by Europeans living near the Mediterranean Sea.

The inventors of the compass used a thin magnet made from a piece of lodestone or iron. They may have hung the magnet from a piece of string. They may have let the magnet float in a bowl of water. They knew that one end of the magnet would always point north no matter which way they turned.

Explorers and travelers used these early compasses to help find their way at sea or in places on land where there were no roads.

People made better compasses by putting a card under the magnet. The card showed the directions of north, south, east, and west. People could tell which way they were going by looking at the magnet and the directions on the card. This type of compass helped keep people from getting lost.

CHAPTER THREE

A MYSTERIOUS FORCE

Hold a refrigerator magnet very close to your refrigerator door. Now let it go. The magnet jumps across empty space and sticks to the refrigerator. How can this be?

Try this experiment with a different kind of magnet. Hold a bar magnet or horseshoe magnet over some iron nails. The nails jump up to the magnet. Jumping nails might seem like magic. The nails jump because magnets have a force that pulls or pushes. The force comes from their north and south poles.

Look closely at two bar magnets. On each magnet, one end should have an *N* and the other end should have an *S.* These letters stand for north and south poles. Put the north pole of one magnet against the south pole of the other magnet. See how they stick together?

Opposite poles of magnets attract each other and will stick together.

If you look closely at the iron filings on the ends of these magnets you can tell that the two poles are alike and are pushing away from each other.

Now bring the south poles of both magnets together. See how they try to push away from each other?

The north pole of one magnet always pulls toward the south pole of another magnet. The south pole of one magnet always pushes away from the south pole of another magnet. The north poles of magnets also push away from each other.

The pull of north and south magnetic poles is what makes refrigerator magnets jump to refrigerator doors. It is what makes nails jump up to horseshoe and bar magnets.

CHAPTER FOUR

THE FORCE AROUND A MAGNET

The pull of north and south poles is strongest if the magnets are close together. Test the pull of a refrigerator magnet. Bring the magnet close enough to jump to the refrigerator door. Now move it farther and farther away. Let go of the magnet each time. When it is far enough away, the magnet will not jump. It will just fall to the floor.

You can also feel the magnetic attraction between bar magnets. Hold the north and south poles of two bar magnets far apart. Slowly bring them closer together. When they are close enough, you will feel the two magnets trying to pull together. This pulling comes from magnetic force. The pattern of force around a magnet is sometimes called a **magnetic field.** As you get further away from a magnet,

*If this boy holds the refrigerator magnet far enough away from the refrigerator
door, it will drop to the floor instead of sticking to the refrigerator.*

the magnetic field gets weaker. You cannot see magnetic fields. You

can only see and feel what a magnetic field does.

Picture a magnetic field as being many looping lines. The lines

start at the north pole of a magnet. They loop out from the

magnet and go back in at the south pole. The lines are close

together at the north and south poles. The force of a magnet

is strongest at its poles.

You can make a magnet "draw" its magnetic field. Put a piece

of paper on top of a bar magnet. Then sprinkle tiny bits of iron

called filings on top of the paper. The filings will line up around

the magnet in the shape of the magnetic field.

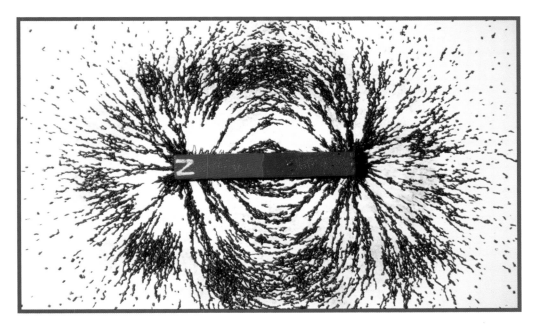

*Iron filings sprinkled around a bar magnet will arrange themselves
in a pattern that shows the magnet's magnetic field.*

If a magnet it strong enough, it can even lift people!

Strong magnets have big magnetic fields. Weak magnets have small magnetic fields. The pulling power of a strong magnet goes out farther than the pulling power of a weak magnet. A stronger bar magnet can jump across a greater distance to your refrigerator door than a weaker refrigerator magnet.

MAGNETS IN SPACE

Did you know that there are huge magnets in outer space? Earth and some of the other planets are giant magnets. They are surrounded by magnetic fields.

The Sun and other stars are also huge magnets. The Sun's magnetic field seems very strange. It goes in and out of the Sun and loops far out into space. The Sun's mag-netic field can cause magnetic storms on Earth. Magnetic storms can damage satellites orbiting above Earth and can even cause power surges that can damage computers on Earth.

Particles streaming off the Sun can get trapped in Earth's magnetic field. This makes eerie lights dance across the far northern and

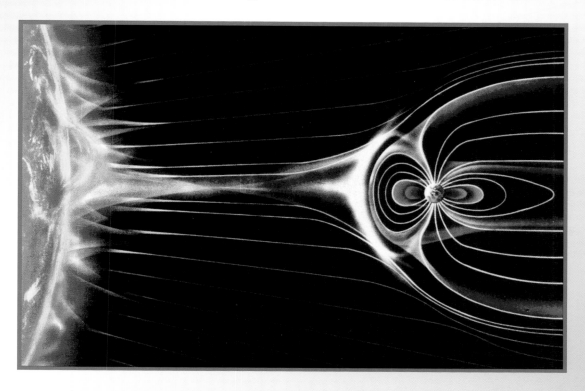

southern skies. The lights are red or green or blue and sometimes even pink and violet. They are called auroras.

Here is an interesting fact about Magnet Earth. Because Earth is a magnet, it has magnetic north and south poles. It also has geographic North and South poles. The North Pole is at the top of Earth in the Arctic Circle. The South Pole is at the bottom of Earth in the Antarctic.

The north pole of a bar magnet always points toward the north. Why? This is kind of a trick question. Remember, the north pole of one magnet always pulls toward the south pole of another magnet.

Here is the tricky part of the answer: The north pole of a bar magnet points north because Earth's *magnetic* south pole is near its *geographic* North Pole. Earth's magnetic north pole is near its geographic South Pole. Earth's north and south magnetic poles seem to us like they are upside down!

CHAPTER FIVE

MAKING MAGNETS

The only natural magnet that exists is lodestone. All other magnets must be made. Long ago, people learned that rubbing iron with lodestone turns the iron into a magnet. How does this work?

Everything is made of **atoms**. Atoms are much too small for you to see. The period at the end of this sentence is made of billions of atoms. The atoms in a piece of iron tend to group together to form tiny magnets. These tiny magnets are called domains. They are so small that there are millions of them in a piece of iron as big as the magnets you may have seen at home or at school.

The tiny magnets in a piece of iron point every which way. Rubbing the iron with a piece of lodestone makes many of the tiny magnets line up. Rubbing makes many of the north poles in the tiny magnets point the same way. When enough of these poles point the same way, the whole piece of iron becomes a magnet.

You can make a magnet by touching certain metals with a magnet. The magnetic field makes many of the tiny magnets in a piece of metal line up in the same direction. Turning a metal into a magnet is called magnetization.

Electricity can also make magnets. These kinds of magnets are called electromagnets. Powerful electromagnets are made of electric wires wrapped around pieces of iron or steel.

You can make your own simple electromagnet. You need a battery, an iron nail, and some copper wire. Wrap the copper wire around the iron nail many times. Then connect one end of the wire to the positive end of the battery. Connect the other end of

Powerful electromagnets are used in scrap metal yards to move heavy objects around.

the wire to the negative end of the battery. If you place some

paper clips near the nail, it will pick them up. The electric current

flowing through the copper wire has created a magnet.

You can make your own electromagnet with a battery, some copper wire, and an iron nail.

Most magnets today are made in factories. Workers melt

mixtures of metals, such as aluminum, nickel, cobalt, iron, and

copper. They pour the liquid mixtures into molds. An electro-

magnet around the mold sets up a magnetic field. The metals

cool and harden inside

the magnetic field.

This makes many of

the tiny magnets

in the metals

line up in the

same direction.

Magnets

molded from mix-

tures of metals are

Metals are melted in foundries and poured into molds to make many things. Most magnets are made from mixtures of metals that are melted and poured into molds that are surrounded by an electromagnetic field. As the metal mixture cools and hardens, a magnet is created.

permanent magnets. The metals in a permanent magnet

"remember" that they were magnetized.

Other magnets are **temporary** magnets. They "forget" that

they were magnetized.

CHAPTER SIX

USING MAGNETS

Scientists in the 1800s learned that there is a link between electricity and magnetism. They also learned that magnets could be used to make electric motors. Electric motors have parts that move.

The motors usually contain electromagnets that are made of coils of wire wrapped around iron **cores.** The electromagnets make a part in the motor move. The moving part makes the motor work.

Electric motors are everywhere in your home and

A factory worker makes parts that will be used to make electromagnets.

school. Electric motors drive sewing machines, refrigerators, vacuum cleaners, food processors, washing machines, fans, and hair dryers. Some ships and trains run on electric motors. Everything that has an electric motor uses magnetism.

Some magnets are used for lifting. There are huge electromagnets in steel mills. These magnets lift big pieces of iron and steel. Big electromagnets in junkyards can pick up whole cars.

Magnetic tape stores sounds and pictures. You listen to music on magnetic audiotape. You watch movies on magnetic videotape. Your computer uses magnetism to store your homework and your computer games on a disk drive.

Doctors use a machine with powerful magnets to see inside the human body. Taking pictures inside the body using magnets and radio waves is called Magnetic Resonance Imaging (MRI).

The pushing force of powerful magnets make maglev trains—such as this one in Germany—run.

A new kind of train, called a maglev train, uses magnets to float in the air. Maglev is short for magnetic **levitation.** A maglev train uses the pushing force of mag-nets—the force that makes two north or south poles push away from each other. There are powerful magnets in the train. There are powerful magnets in the track. The magnets push away from each other and lift the train up. Then the train moves along without touching the track.

Scientists are still learning new things about magnetism. Inventors continue to look for new ways to use magnets to make life easier.

MAGNETS IN ANIMALS

Every year, many animals migrate, or travel, from one place to another. Some animals go north for summer and south for winter. They may make round trips that cover thousands of miles. Swarms of monarch butterflies travel from Canada and the northern United States to spend the winter in places as far south as Mexico.

Some whales and fish swim across the open sea. One kind of sea turtle finds its way between South America and a tiny island in the middle of the Atlantic Ocean.

Every autumn, flocks of ducks and geese fly overhead. They travel south for the winter. Some are making a journey of thousands of miles.

Arctic terns are migrating birds that cover up to 35,400 kilometers (22,000 miles) every year.

How do animals find their way? Biologists think that some animals use the position of the sun and the stars to help tell where they are going. Some animals may see or even smell landmarks to find their way.

Many biologists now think that some animals have a built-in compass. They think that certain birds, insects, fish, and other sea animals have tiny bits of magnetic material in their bodies. The tiny magnets line up along Earth's magnetic field. Somehow the animals use these compasses inside their bodies to find their way over thousands of miles.

GLOSSARY

atoms (AT-ums) Atoms are tiny bits of matter that make up everything in the universe.

cores (KORS) Cores are the center parts of things.

levitation (lev-uh-TAY-shun) Levitation is the act of floating above the ground or another object.

lodestone (LOHD-stohn) Lodestone is rock made of the mineral magnetite that acts as a natural magnet.

magnetic field (mag-NET-ik FEELD) A magnetic field is the area around a magnet in which the magnet's pull or push can be detected.

magnetic materials (mag-NET-ik muh-TIHR-ee-ulz) Magnetic materials are materials that are attracted to or pulled toward a magnet.

mineral (MIN-ur-uhl) A mineral is a material found in nature that is not a plant or an animal.

nonmagnetic materials (non-mag-NET-ik muh-TIHR-ee-ulz) Nonmagnetic materials are materials that are not pulled toward a magnet.

particles (PAR-tuh-kuhls) Particles are tiny pieces of something.

permanent (PUR-muh-nuhnt) Something that is permanent is meant to last for a long time.

temporary (TEM-puh-rar-ee) Something that is temporary will only last for a short time.

▶ You can demagnetize a magnet by hitting it with a hammer or dropping it on the floor. You can also heat a magnet to demagnetize it.

▶ Some ancient people believed there were magnetic islands made of lodestone. They thought the islands pulled on the iron nails in ships. They used this belief to explain why ships disappeared mysteriously at sea.

▶ Some bacteria have tiny magnets inside them.

▶ In 1820, a Danish scientist named Hans Christian Oersted (1777–1851) found a link between electricity and magnetism by bringing an electric wire close to a compass. The electric current in the wire caused the compass needle to move.

▶ Magnetism has no known harmful effects on human beings, although doctors do not perform MRIs on pregnant women because they are uncertain about the possible effects on unborn babies.

▶ If you break a magnet in half, each piece will have a north and south magnetic pole. No matter how many pieces you break a magnet into, each piece will have a north pole and a south pole. It is not possible to end up with only one pole.

▶ Some metals such as bismuth are actually repelled by magnets and are called diamagnetic.

▶ Some metals are attracted to magnets, such as iron, cobalt, and nickel. Other metals, such as aluminum, copper, silver, and gold, are not attracted to magnets.

▶ A U.S. five-cent coin, or nickel, will not be attracted to a magnet. This is because the coin is mostly made of copper.

TIMELINE

circa A.D. 1000   The Chinese discover that a piece of lodestone floating on water will always point north and south.

1600   William Gilbert (top left), the physician to Queen Elizabeth I of England, discovers that Earth is a giant magnet and writes a paper on the uses and properties of magnetism.

1724   George Graham in England and Anders Celsius in Sweden discover magnetic storms, disturbances in Earth's atmosphere that cause compasses to temporarily point in different directions.

1750   John Mitchell discovers that the two poles of a magnet are equal in strength.

1819   French physicist Andre Marie Ampere and Danish physicist Hans Christian Oersted (right) prove that electricity and magnetism are related.

1830s   English scientist Michael Faraday and American physicist Joseph Henry both discover that a changing magnetic field creates an electric current in a coil of wire.

1864   Scottish scientist James Clerk Maxwell (bottom left) uses mathematics to describe the laws of electricity and magnetism.

1900s   Physicists develop a theory to explain how magnetism works inside atoms.

1901   Using equipment that makes use of magnets, Guglielmo Marconi successfully sends radio signals across the Atlantic Ocean.

1930s   American physicist Francis Bitter makes magnets strong enough to use for scientific research.

1970s   Scientists make magnets powerful enough to lift maglev trains.

HOW TO LEARN MORE ABOUT MAGNETISM

At the Library

Bryant-Mole, Karen. *Magnets.* Chicago: Heinemann Library, 2002.

Cooper, Jason. *Magnets.* Vero Beach, Fla.: Rourke Publishing, 2003.

Riley, Peter D. *Magnets.* Milwaukee.: Gareth Stevens, 2002.

Royston, Angela. *Magnetic and Nonmagnetic.* Chicago: Heinemann Library, 2003.

Schreiber, Anne, and Adrian C. Sinnott (illustrator).
Magnets. New York: Grosset & Dunlap, 2003.

On the Web

VISIT OUR HOME PAGE FOR LOTS OF LINKS ABOUT MAGNETISM:
http://www.childsworld.com/links.html
Note to Parents, Teachers, and Librarians: We routinely verify our Web links to make
sure they're safe, active sites—so encourage your readers to check them out!

Places to Visit or Contact

IMAGINATION STATION
To tour the exhibit on Electricity and Magnetism
224 East Nash Street
Wilson, NC 27894
252/291-5113

NATIONAL HIGH MAGNETIC FIELD LABORATORY
*To write for more information about the
educational programs offered by the Magnet Lab*
1800 East Paul Dirac Drive
Tallahassee, FL 32310
850/644-0311

INDEX

About the Author

Darlene R. Stille is a science writer. She has lived in Chicago, Illinois, all her life. When she was in high school, she fell in love with science. While attending the University of Illinois she discovered that she also loved writing. She was fortunate to find a career that allowed her to combine both her interests. Darlene Stille has written more than 60 books for young people.